THE

ELEPHANTOM

IN

THE

ROOM

a psychological tail

THE

ELEPHANTOM

IN THE ROOM

a psychological tail

Nuru

The Elephantom in the Room
a psychological tail

3rd Edition

Copyright ©2018 by Nuru

Any members of educational institutions wishing to photocopy part or all of the

work for classroom use, or publishers who would like to obtain permission

to include the work in an anthology, should send their inquiries to

Dabs & Company

22200 W. 11 Mile Rd.

Unit 502

Southfield, MI

48037-0502, USA

(313) 451-2628

dabsandco@gmail.com

This is a work of fiction.
Situations, places and incidents either are the product of the
author's imagination or are used fictitiously.

Please Note

"Strong Language" is used throughout the Story

The characters are engaging in "code-switching". They are using both standard English and Black English, at times even in the same sentence. Also, more than one way to pronounce or use a word is shown.

If you have difficulty understanding their speech,

try reading the story aloud!

THE ELEPHANTOM IN THE ROOM

a psychological tail

"You're obsessed, you know."

"Not. I am merely trying to keep from having Post Traumatic Stress Disorder."

"PTSD? Have you been taking your medication?"

"Fuck you — I mean — fuck that. Why do you always go there when you don't like what I'm saying?

"That's because you are obsessing."

"My issues have nothing to do with obsession. YOU'RE the self-professed control freak. Anyway, talk is therapeutic AND cathartic…"

"Maybe for you but not the listener. Unless they're a paid professional."

"Well, mine's also a caring individual. I don't think it's just about the Bens with him. ANY—T—WAY, I'll give you a break. You're soooo not trying to be empathetic. Howsomever, your ability to block out what you don't want to deal with IS impressive. All of us can't do that. Doesn't mean we're damaged – just more sensitive. Price one pays for being gifted, you know."

I smirk as I leave my cousin before she can turn the cold shoulder. She had already shut down. Kinda sad. I listen to her rant when she needs to. I even encourage her. One of her friends told her rehashing crap does more harm than good. Keeps ME from killing many a MoFo! A conscious practice to totally ignore shit that's getting on my last-frayed-nerve. Even if it seems effortless, it's a gift but not a solution.

I call Gem, a friend who's always ready to commiserate. She's had some serious shit to deal with in her life to the point where she's liable to go into a tirade about almost anything. Raw as a uncooked turnip. Well, I like eatin raw turnips. They're sweet once you get past the thick coverin. An good for you too. Just like my friend. She wouldn't have had to become so tough if it wasn't for the slings n arrows bullshit. Damn! I'm cussin a lot lately. Even for me. "Yo, gurl. What it be?"

"Hey. Nothin but a thang. Didn't get much sleep last night. Not likely to get much tonight, either."

"SOS for you. Wish I could help." She's a crusader rabbit with mighty muscle … usually.

"Yeah, I know. Same here. Socks'll be over to clumsily give me a mess-ag-itate. Lease that'll help me loosen up some. Wish he'd go to school an learn how."

"Your masseur du jour. Love is always inadequate in some way. Um, was tryin to make my cuz understand why I can't "just move on." Why do folk always put "just" in front of hard stuff they expect you to "just" do? Nike an shit. A victory doesn't have to happen instantaneously. Hell, if things was JUST, wouldn't nobody have to move on."

Gem chuckles hoarsely. She can't kick the cigs even though they kickin her ass.

Dang, I need to be writin. Whenever I start riffin an connectin invisible dots, I know it's time to drain my brain.

"So, you still tryin to do the *impossible*,"

Gem spits it French stylee. A language I'd like to learn. An Spanish, an …

"You need to bury that horse," she deadpans.

"It's hard cuz you wanna share stuff witcho fam. I try to make her see how everybody got to deal wit crap the way THEY got to. She's had her share an always bounces back. But I can tell the toll has been takin her because it manifests in her phySICKly, which I am NOT tryin to have. She goes hard an drops hard when she can. Self-induced mania," *An shit*, I add mentally.

Gem exhales an spaces out for a minute. I try not to ask if she's still there but I do. I am overly conscious about how LOQUACIOUS I can be. Once I get started, it easily morphs into a lecture. Sometimes even stand up comedy. The latter goes down easier… usually. "I know, you're thinkin the pot an the kettle. But I hate seein folk I care bout sufferin an can't help em. Yes, I—resist—letting—folk—see—me—weak—and—need—help—my—own—damn—self," Mantramatically.

That's anotha thing I do: mentally an verbally relate everything back to me an my experiences. Makes me seem ALL EGO to most but it's the

way I think; the way I understand things an wanna help others process what they puzzlin about. Who doesn't go wit what they know? I can tell I help but most don't like gettin straight to the heart of the matter. Makes them have to look within. They'd rather keep strugglin an basically only want a sympathetic soundin board.
I'm more like a mirror.

"Oh, fuck," Gem mumbles. "I forgot to take ANYTHING out for dinner. DAMMIT!"

I go into helpful mode: "You got some salad? Just put some tuna or somethin on it an you got a meal."

"It's kinda wilted. OK. So, feelin way better now that you free?"

"HELL to the YEAH! Be glad when I get everything settled. Here AND THERE."

I was "living" in a former friend's house for years. We'd known each other for almost ten before. He is a BIG dude, makes a trumpet sound when he stretches, has a phenomenal memory, an loves peanuts. So, of course, his nickname is Elephant.
Weeell, I. Had. No. Idea. Negro got a PhD in GASLIGHTING.

I lost my main job out of two. Found out AFTER my contract renewal was allowed to drop. No warning. Boss believed a lie. Told me later: "I guess I should have talked to you first." NO FUCKIN SHIT? Four years later, I had to say goodbye to MY big-ass apartment.

Elephant generously offered to let me rent from him. We were getting along fine. None of his intermittent girlfriends – or boyfriends –

seemed to have a problem with me being around. I basically kept to myself — anyway — even though he wanted me to give him more attention. But I was wrapped up in my lack of a steady job and income and writing the great un-American novel. I did try to be more social with him, even though he would usually walk away to show me he DIDN'T need me an stuff. Baby-ass tit-for-tat shit.

After a few years I don't know which of us wanted me gone first. If he did, I didn't get the memo. I think I became toast cuz I didn't fulfill his need to feel superior an magnanimous after havin SAVED me. Had to remind him I HAVE a mother AND ALWAYS some modicum of self-esteem — unless I'm reeeeaaaally depressed.

I was still heavily grieving the loss of my father, loss of the job two months after, an sliding the slow, slippery slope of losing a place where you lived for almost nine years, having to sell and give away what couldn't be kept or put in storage. Elephant seemed to resent that. In his opinion, my dejection and perceived lack of relief meant I had breached the code of the Promised Land, even as I reached it. My thankfulness and appreciation weren't getting it.

I was eventually able to get jobs. But keepin one was not doable. Since I was havin so much trouble tryin to work — actually HAD AND LOST two serious opportunity positions that would've utilized both my creative AND administrative sides — I applied for disability. I had to hire a take-charge, aggressive, sharky attorney to get it since I was denied the first time due to SOP. Gettin SSD helped me function a little better by knowin I'd have some kind of income an health bennies I could count on. I paid Elephant all of the money I owed him when I got my lump sum, despite his tellin me I could take my time. Hindsight says he wanted to always keep the upper foot. So, when things got really strange enough for me to notice: a plethora of lies, set-ups, puttin both of us in danger out of spite, etc., I point-blank asked him if he wanted me out. Bein the passive-aggressive, narcissistic, anti-social, psychotic, borderline, histrionic mess I later learned he was: he would never tell me yes or no. Like I had applied for a damn job an was waitin for a decision or some shit. Instead, he covertly upped his game of throwin me off mine. Retrospection: I should've run screamin from the house with just the clothes on my back. But unexpected, expensive, serious stuff — out of my control — had happened before an continued to happen just about the time I was plannin to make my break. I mean, from one year to the next: THREE SURGERIES, FOOD POISONING, A CAR ACCIDENT, and the latest: SEVERE STRESS THAT MIMICKED A HEART ATTACK. All entailed me going to the hospital. Those times were when I realized I REALLY did not like Elephant anymore, in ANY way. Somethin about bein dependent and in a hospital with a fake-ass "friend" pretending to care. I could barely look at the mopey-faced MoFo. Then I'd recall how we used to enjoy each other's company goin out to eat and stuff. And — how after a while — the thrill was DEAD.

I gave my therapists, internist, and psychiatrist each a letter I'd written about what was happening. Shrink immediately told me to get out of the house. Offered me pills to help me get through the crap. I asked my psycho-therapist — does that title mean he crazy AND a rapist? Ha, ha! — to let him know I felt I needed to be as hyper-vigilant as possible, so, "no, thank you." I now had a paper trail in case something was to happen to me.

I was wonderin why I was still in such a situation. What was my reward? To start off, I really didn't notice how I overlooked and rarely commented on Elephant's shitty behavior. I was — unfortunately — used to being around openly dysfunctional people. Sometimes I'm one. So, I'd only make a comment or a mental note of the catalyst and move on. This WAS NOT the desired reaction. Could it be that I was marveling at the phenomena and getting a slight sadistic charge from it? Watching the fucked up spectacle of self-hatred turned outward? A creature totally devoid of empathy? I KNOW I have a vivid imagination and am extremely sensitive to my surrounds but this behavior was carefully orchestrated and would have rendered a weaker person into a Jello pudding pop. It was macabre, yet beautiful in its deliberateness. Like the scene from Silence of the Lambs where Dr. Hannibal Lechter has artfully eviscerated and hung a guard up for display, his abdominal skin furled to the side in the bird-like cage Lechter had been forced to live in. You had to give the guy credit for being a creative. Elephant was also creative and excellent at finding a place for everything and putting EVERYTHING in its PREDETERMINED place.

I felt as if I were on display many times. A rat in a maze. A fish in a bowl. Toyed with, glowered at, hated. A living reminder of failed Pygmalionesque attempts at control.

Even though I was able to turn it all back on Elephant, his mission and self-aggrandizement would not allow him to see when HE was being played. So, I guess he was having some success at getting to my baser nature, helping me to become as miserable as he and as abusive. To sink me to his level and "make" me need him to lift me up. Honestly, I still don't know what kept me there. The only thing I can think of that may have been the cause was that I was — and STILL am — TIRED. Tired of upheaval, stress an strife. Feeling out of control of MY OWN LIFE! I was not ready to deal with moving. I could barely pack a bag to visit fam out-of-state. Change, disruption, an harsh introspection kept me off center. I wanted a FUCKING BREAK from everything! All I wanted to do was write and read in peace. I wanted to recuperate from a break-up, breakdown, lost opportunities, losing my dad, and MY full freedom. I thought I could tough it out but the stress of winning the never ending fight was too great.

   It had never occurred to me — until I began to pay even closer attention — that my misfortunes are Elephant's joys. But my resilience is his bane. And I know that. I think I always knew he did not wish me well but felt I was being negative and repressed it. There was always the bad feeling about us having the same boss who dropped me on a whim. Did he know she was going to? Would he have warned me? Did he actually have a tinge of guilt? Was he anticipating a sideshow of the captive bird in a cage with a cat watching and circling. Meowing plaintively, then yowling menacingly. Climbing, pouncing and deliberately missing.
I know why the caged bird kills.

   Guess I'd gone quiet too long. Gem growls, with extreme prejudice:

   "Fuck that elephant gaslightin psycho muthafucka."

   A true friend. Always knows what to say. "Yep. I'm almost there."
Have to shake the hatred I had begun to feel. I never did want to fulfill that goal of his. I know he is to be pitied but I have come pretty close to wiping that notion out. He truly cannot help himself. I don't believe it is in him to change. I continue, "But — the bastard MADE sure you noticed

him even if you didn't say NOTHIN! Didn't nobody but you an Ruki really WANTED to see his ass all up in the middle of the room. 'Got no time to count my sheep today.'" I break into song. Gem joins in. We sound like folk singin in a raucous bar. Hmmmm ... an elephant in the "middle of the room." Is that what the Spinners was singin bout?

Everybody but Ruki and Gem — acts like I'm paranoid. Even my bud Bowman who likes talkin bout how you ain paranoid if they out to getchu, wit his caw-razy butt. Luckily, ALL my doctors an therapists paid attention to what I suspected. Who in the hell thought to name a job which — if treated as a compound word — becomes "the rapist." Maybe cuz they fuckin witcho mind an YOU PAYIN THEM TO DO IT?. Anyway, they took me seriously when I diagnosed the bit—, heifer, bizastard. That's funny, I'm tryin to stop callin stuff bitch cuz it's sexist but callin folk heifer ain seen as so bad. Both female. So, I guess Elephant was in a animal genus all his own. If I call him a dog, it'd probly be taken as a compliment. Hmmmm. Can a elephant be bi-sexual? I think I remember somethin bout how they play an the male hangs out with his boys longer than he does wit the girls. My pachyderm seems to do the same thang. *Pachy-derm*. Wow. Jus wow.

Yeah, real glad my care professionals respected my opinion. I knew gaslighting-type stress was insidious once I realized it WAS keepin me discombobulated. Could be a lot of testin and medication I was given — when I was really feelin out of it — was due to some psychosomatic bullshit. Now, I was gettin healed after lettin loose! Doin a lot of writin and publishin, workin on puttin things I had scattered all over my room back where they belonged, and feelin light and energetic. All that just from THOROUGHLY tellin Elephant off for the first time.

"No such thing as writer's block. Just temporary constipation," I drolled aloud. Where'd I get that from?

"An shit," Gem co-signed. "But later."

We laugh again.

"Hyper-vigilance CAN be extremely productive. Gives one great material to rein in and write about. Glad I didn't take the 'prevention pills' my psychiatrist offered."

"PILLS TO MAKE IT EASIER? Shit, your ass needed to stay pissed just for the momentum, alone. Pound down some Five Hour Energy an shit. Did you ever see the movie? It was around nineteen-forty-somethin with Ingrid Bergman.

"1944. I don't remember. I just knew the term was coined after the movie. Man tryin to drive his wife crazy by doin crazy shit, right? It's listed in the DSM. At lease it WAS. Sposed to have been a lot of changes in the latest edition. Like, if you identify as no sexual orientation in particular, now you got "gender dysphoria" … an stuff. Re-po-bully-cans. An older copy of a Merck Manual a doctor gave me is helpful. Found out what some weird arthritis-related disease my father had before his doctor (quack, quack) just by looking through it. I believe in doing research. So, when I kept having issues like getting sick an in the emergency room for no APPARENT physical reason, that got me really ready to bounce! I had already started readin up on personality disorders an found all a what I'm sure are Elephant's. Now I wonder how that bit— asshole is able to walk upright! Has he been able to mask the one that is INCURABLE from HIS mind raper? Messin wit my belongins AND my food? Maybe the food poisoning WADN'T from the restaurant! LAWSUIT!"

"Too bad you didn't have a witness to somma that shit."

"Oh, but I did. The gremlins that were around when the things occurred. Never could find they asses, though. B-U-T-T — ha, ha, Elephant's ASS is classic textbook. I wrote a note asking him to quit pouring out my expensive health drink that I'd take a sip of everyday. It had gone from 6/6 to 5/6 in less than a month. He had claimed the need for me to write some things down so he could fully understand what I meant. So, I figured that was a good time to do so. Came to me later and asked "Why would I do that?" GUUURL! I'ma shonuff survivor!"

"That's fo DAMN sho! You lookin more relaxed, got all your belongings in one place, you ain gotta worry about your privacy bein violated anymore, an whatever that fool was doin to your stuff and you. I knew it was over when he poked a hole in the corner of that thick-ass plastic bottle you had, IN. THE. CORNER. WITH. A. SHARP. OBJECT!!! Had to have taken at least two minutes to do. That bastard was escalatin fast an shit."

We both say "an shit" together an laugh. Rehearsed.

"Remember I had to go see a dermatologist about my right eye lookin funny and a sudden large cyst on my side?"

"Yeah, I remember how your eye looked but not about the cyst."

"Well, of course they couldn't find any reason for either. I don't have to have the cyst removed because it went down an was told my eye was probably changin because I was "getting older". Better than bein poisoned."

"Medical Mystery Tour an shit."

"Well, the bastard still made a dent in my armor. Now he's turned from jus havin been in the room to a FUCKIN PHANTOM. Still doggin me. But I'ma make him like GHOST!"

We both found comic relief by imitatin P-Funk with a new version of a fav song of mine: "Now I lay me down to sleep … GASLIGHT!" Then it's bust a gut time.

I love havin good friends who understand why I can't JUST shake the ElePHANTOM. Ha, ha. A lot of us black folk don't say phantom right. Comes out like "fanthom", just like "liberry". Most linguists say it's a hard thing to change. I thought bout makin that my major in college once. I'ma lingo lover an gangsta quipsta sista as are most of my buds.

Gem an I finally stop laughin an she signs off after sayin good night. I try to sound as sincere as she does when I say it back. It wadn't a habit in my family growin up. Sayin good mornin wadn't big, either. Seems to me we just made eye contact an grunted when seein each other for the first time that day. I think we just drifted away at bedtime except when we kids had to be told to go.

I survey the unpacked boxes – symbols of uncharacteristic disorganization and my overdue hasty decision to BOOK OUT! Hah! Most got books I can't part wit in em.

I clock time an sigh. I call Ruki-kabuki — who's probly STILL up — cause I STILL need a fix. She been through the same fire — only worse — and just about as bad as Gem.

Compared to their sufferin, mine was peanuts.

An shit.

★

Gaslighting Behavior and Other Disorders

Gaslighting

A form of intimidation or psychological abuse, sometimes called
Ambient Abuse where false information is presented to the victim,
making them doubt their own memory, perception and quite often,
their sanity. The classic example of gaslighting is to switch something
around on someone that you know they're sure to notice, but then
deny knowing anything about it, and to explain that they "must be
imagining things" when they challenge these changes.
~ Urban Dictionary

Narcissistic Personality Disorder

Persons diagnosed with a Narcissistic Personality Disorder are
characterized by unwarranted feelings of self-importance. They have a
sense of entitlement and demonstrate grandiosity in their beliefs and
behavior. They have a strong need for admiration, but lack feelings of
empathy for others. These qualities are usually defenses against a deep
feeling of inferiority and of being unloved.

Personality Traits

An individual whose self-esteem was severely arrested during
childhood, who usually displays major paranoid tendencies, and who
holds on to an illusion of omnipotence. These people are fighting
delusions of insignificance and lost value, and trying to re-establish
their self-esteem through grandiose fantasies and self-reinforcement.
When unable to gain recognition or support from others, they take on
the role of a heroic or worshiped person with a grandiose mission.
~ Wikipedia

THE ELEPHANTOM IN THE ROOM   by Nuru   copyright © 2018

Histrionic Personality Disorder

 Antisocial, narcissistic, borderline, and histrionic personality disorders
are all closely related since they all share the same core feature of
antagonism. This core feature is an exaggerated sense of self-
importance, insensitivity towards the feelings and needs of others, and
callous exploitation of others. These antagonistic behaviors put the
individual at odds with other people. If an individual has one of these
antagonistic personality disorders, they are very likely to have another.
~ Internet Mental Health

About the Behaviors of "Elephant"

The method of Gaslighting is a serious attempt to do — usually, only —
psychological harm to another.

If the person is skilled at the behavior, they can make life miserable and
frightening for the victim.

The victim must try to be strong and trust their own feelings and learn
ways to handle the abuser. It would be best for the abused to remove
themselves from the situation. It may not be possible to continue a
positive relationship with the abuser — even from a distance.

Following are some ways to recognize a person using some controlling
and/or entrapment techniques. The person usually presents with other
disorders including — but not limited to — narcissism.

These suggestions are geared toward recognizing through
understanding the hidden motives. They are mostly referring to a more
developed relationship such as with a relative, boss, or long time

acquaintance. The following suggestions may not be adequate for your situation.

Know that something about you has attracted this person(s). They have chosen you based on what they need from you. They want you in their world for validation of their desirability. You may have even initiated the relationship based on your empathy radar for helping others and feeling you have much to offer. Feeling *genuine* concern about someone else's well-being means you are not a narcissist, as well as believing you can help without planning to exploit, may have kept you from becoming one.

Narcissists are made, not born.

(Recent genetic discoveries may prove otherwise.)

IMPORTANT!

The following are ONLY SUGGESTIONS.

SEEK PROFESSIONAL HELP if necessary.

If you suspect you are in serious danger, remove yourself ASAP!

Three Signs You May Be Dealing With a Narcissistic Abuser

YOU ARE BEING APPROACHED BY A PERSON WHO

1. ... Flatters You Excessively

Trust your senses when someone who doesn't know you personally – but seems to know much about you – begins telling you how great you are and profusely complimenting you for characteristics and abilities you may have and don't have. An example: You are a good dancer but a would-be Narcissistic Abuser gushes about how wonderfully you light up the dance floor whenever you're on it. Show the stranger mild appreciation but pay close attention to what is being said. Is the information readily available through social media or some other potentially public source? If you decide to become friends keep things even. Don't accept their always paying for meals, giving you gifts, etc. even after you've known them for a bit. That will later become fodder for attempts to make you feel beholden and ungrateful. During early "courtship" you'll rarely be admonished or challenged for any flaws or faults in you or the relationship. You may have been duped into believing you are going to benefit from having one with a seemingly charming, generous, like-minded individual. So it's necessary to put your own needs in perspective. What is it that allows you to feel so welcoming toward someone your don't know personally? What are you expecting from a relationship with them? The Narcissistic Abuser will patiently extract, nurse and exploit that need.

They are looking forward to corrupting you so they no longer have to look up to you.

DEFENSE:

Observe the possibly Narcissistic Abuser's attempts to get close to you by showering you with praise. Don't believe in their words or overly react to them. Thank them for the compliments and give them a bit of a chance to convince you they are indeed a Narcissistic Abuser. Set boundaries and see if they frequently cross them. Note the growth of their effusive behaviors. Are they mirroring yours and claiming to be a fan of things you enjoy? Do you feel as if they are trying to impress you as if you are on a first date? Stop the merry-go-round and assess your feelings. If you are uncomfortable make any excuse and get away from them as soon as possible so you may right your equilibrium! If you are unable to remove yourself from their presence immediately, make a phone call (You can make a non-call by turning your phone OFF and be free to say anything you want into it.), send a text, begin reading a physical piece of paper or e-book, say you are very tired and need to go home, engage in a conversation with another person without including the possible Narcissistic Abuser. These things will slow their roll and rhythm and allow you to take a break without seeming weak. That may discourage a Narcissistic Abuser because they don't want to have to "work" in order to regain attention or be included. They especially hate to be ignored or disparaged in any way, anywhere. The Narcissistic Abuser may decide to punish you by not seeking inclusion and walking away from you as in *It's your loss*. However, don't be surprised if they approach you again for another try. Express to the possible Narcissistic Abuser how you seem to attract people who want to use you and you can always tell when it's happening. You haven't accused the possible Narcissistic Abuser of doing it, so that prevents an argument and may discourage another attempt.

The above tactics may stop a Narcissistic Abuser in their tracks. But if you've been involved in a relationship with the person, try using a less overt and obvious manner. Triggering past hurts, self-hatred or embarrassments will likely cause you to become an even more desirable target. Narcissistic Abusers thrive on observing your emotions and behaviors as they can be used for application of future manipulation and mistreatment. They relish the challenge of the hunt. It will be easier to allow them to "desert" you due to boredom.

If you find yourself ensnared, it doesn't mean you have to succumb.

2. ... is Overly Grateful For Any Positive Attention

The Narcissistic Abuser is on the prowl for truly good and generous people. They are skilled at this and are able to detect and gauge your wants and needs. The Narcissistic Abuser readily accepts your basic kindnesses and praises you highly for them. They tell you how wonderful you have made them feel and are more than willing to receive your tribute. After the Narcissistic Abuser feels they have deceived and somewhat trained you – even if it has taken years – they will continue to reward you in some manner. Following this security they usually begin the phase of belittling any small effort you now make to please them. This may be totally ignoring you, making you the butt of jokes in private and public, refusing to accept unearned apologies, emanating unpleasantness and/or confusing and frightening you. Their ultimate goal is to condition you to want to earn their love and attention after having activated your exclusive concern and desire to help even if it causes you slight inconvenience or more.

Control is paramount and sublime.

DEFENSE:

Tell trusted friends about what is happening. Give them as much information about the Narcissistic Abuser as possible. Continue to feed the Narcissistic Abuser with occasional praise and small kindnesses while planning your escape. Despite their abusive actions they are afraid of losing you. They are worried about your discovering they are insecure, soulless, hate-filled and weak. Their attachment disorder has caused them to depend on you for company and ego boosts. Continue doing a few desired things to keep them feeling in control. They will eventually sense you are breaking away. This is when their neediness fully reveals itself and makes it plain you need to move on without deliberately inflicting unnecessary pain or receiving any. You have become useless to the Narcissistic Abuser once they realize you know who they really are and have nothing left for them to extract. You are now a threat.

You're planning to get-a-way; not to get away with cruelty.

3. ... Is Becoming a Serious Threat

The Narcissistic Abuser is capable of becoming a serious threat at anytime. And this can be said about anyone. But anyone who has made it their business to study you is dangerous.

Set boundaries and see if they frequently cross them. Note the growth of their effusive behaviors. Are they regularly seeking sympathy and leave you feeling guilty because you have trouble feeling any? Are you uncomfortable with any physical contact with them? Do they seem impatient and jealous when you are interacting with others? Do they ridiculously mistreat waitpersons, children and the elderly? Are you uncomfortable being alone with them? Do you feel discarded or on display when their friends and family are on the scene? Do they "leave you hanging"on the phone, waiting for them to take you somewhere or mysteriously disappear without contact for longer and longer periods? Do they seem to be devoid of empathy for others? Do they "playfully" mistreat you in front of others? Do they insert themselves into events involving you where they know they aren't welcome? Do they subject you to people – in public places – they associate with who openly show their dislike of you? Do they stand up for you? Have they tampered with something of yours in a way where you'd know it? Are they able to "innocently" push your "explosive anger button" then calmly ask why you are angry? When you begin to doubt your own negative behavior and thoughts or feel you may act on them, you need to end the relationship ASAP then reclaim and re-adjust your life!

 DEFENSE:

The next steps will be to sever all ties and stay aware. Instruct others – whom you haven't already alerted – to refrain from discussing you for any reason with the Narcissistic Abuser! Of course, you have no control over all others who may know you both. Think of these measures as similar to what great lengths a person must take to hide from an abusive spouse.

If you are fearful of the actions of the Narcissistic Abuser, you have every right to be. Don't feel any shame for that. You have been subjected to a harrowing experience! This is true even if you are a physically and mentally strong survivor.

So … allow yourself to feel victorious!

Apply your new awareness and power to your arsenal of protection.

SUMMARY:

The malignancy of the narcissist is powerful and has a life of its own. But the price is excruciating. To live in fear of being found out for who you really are makes for a horrifying existence. A person who is filled with self-loathing and misery needs to spread it around.

DON'T WAIT FOR THE SHARE.

BE VIGILANT

BE STRONG

BE BRAVE

BE SELF-AWARE

BE REALISTIC

BE COURAGEOUS

BE SAFE

BE WELL

Regarding the Disorders Exhibited in the Story

Although the story is not about a particular person, it is a compilation of negative behaviors I have witnessed over the years, proving to me that there are many people harboring the disorders. If you know someone who exhibits the behaviors and you can't seem to help them, it is because they are very hard to treat. Some are even considered incurable. Even if you decide to get away from the person for your own sanity and safety, remember they are suffering also. Please resist the urge to hurt them in any way. Point them toward help, if possible but do not allow them the chance to mistreat you again.

Be Well!

From the Author

I write and write.

Then I write some more.

My thoughts are constantly at war.

I fight, all right.

Most times some more.

My brain gets drained

Out the words pour!

And I soar!

Enjoy!

~ Nuru

Books by

Dabs & Company

The Magic Pencil Series

~ Karen E. Dabney

The YoungStar Series

~ Karen E. Dabney

Splendor for Your Vendors!

~ Karen E. Dabney

Unhappiness Is ...

~ Karen E. Dabney

Necessary Roughness

~ Safi

Jenga

~ Nuru & Karen E. Dabney

The Elephantom in the Room

~ Nuru & Karen E. Dabney

Soon Come!

Recognize & Revoke Passive Permission

~ Karen E. Dabney